Looking Within…

◈

Beverly Leach
aka
Ruth Ghio

Copyright ©2026 by Beverly Leach aka Ruth Ghio

Arena Press
Grass Valley, CA

Original cover and book design: Adden Design

Cover photo: author's private collection

All rights reserved. This book or any portion thereof may not be reproduced or used in any manner without the express written permission of the author, except for the use of brief quotations in a book review, or as permitted by U.S. copyright law.

ISBN: 979-8-9893956-3-7

Dedicated to my parents
Edna and Ralph Leach
and
Ruth Lambert, my grandmother.
Without these people there would be no story.

I also dedicate this book
to my Finnish relatives and ancestors
who played a larger role
in my development than I imagined.

I also wrote this book for my four children:
Charlotte, Beth, Tony, and Kathy
who were also affected by this story
and may have never known
what in the hell was happening.

Looking Within...

Beverly Leach
aka
Ruth Ghio

Contents

Introduction 15

The Poems

Living and Leaving 18
An Ordinary Day 20
Change 24
Evening 25
Christmas Day 26
Ode to Animals 28
Flying 30
People Here 33
Family 34
Food 36
Chatting with Trees 37
The Gypsy 38
Opossum 40
Woman 43
Meditation 44
Beverly 45
Living 46
When I Plan 47
Polarity 48
The End of the Old 50
Blame and Healing 52
Mystery 54
River Water 56
Birds on Fire 57
Oaxaca 58
Revealing 61

Cake Making—Contact Paper—Alcohol in My Family	62
Poem for Nina	65
Put Back 'Til Next Time	66
Ralph	69
I Give You My Love	70
June	72
Self-Love	74
Welcome	76
Today	77
I-80	78
My Children	80
To Feel a Body's Warmth	82
Maybe It's Time	84
Trapped	86
Black Cat	88
My Son	92
Bingo	94
After Bingo	99
Gifts	100
Ocean	103
Coda and Quinta	104
Tree	106
Joy	109
Clay	110
The Couple	114
Aunt Ethel Aging	118
The Dog Ate My Homework	120
I Walk the Line	121
Along the Silver Altar	122
I Am Water Flowing	124

Dancing Through the Trees 125
Between 126
Rhythms 127
The Poet 128
Words and Language 130
Flame 132
Words 134
The Mouse and the Lion 135
Love 136
The Oldest Sister 138
Love Story 140
I Dreamed I Was a Wild Pony 143
Missing and Forgetting 144
The Black Fedora and Other Things 146
Acknowledgments 151

Poems ...

... from over the years

INTRODUCTION

If you have spent any time at all with Ruth Ghio you may easily come away with the sense that she's an eclectic soul. In conversation, she might say to you, "You know ... I'm really a generalist." Or she might tell you stories about how as a girl, her mind was so active that little "day-to-day" things—like scarves—might get rolled up and put into the refrigerator accidentally because her attention was so far away. Combine this immense curiosity and hunger to understand the ways of the world with the imagination of a child desperate to find a place of safety, and you get the grist for the mill of this volume of poems.

Ruth (then known as Beverly Leach) began living in the world of poetry when, as a small child in North Dakota, she hid in meadows of tall, golden grasses and discovered faces and stories in the clouds drifting across vivid blue skies. From the day she was five and won a poetry prize, she has continued finding solace and joy in the poet's world of language and rhythm.

This volume, *Looking Within...*, contains a rich sampling of her dedication to writing, throughout her long and multifaceted life. Since searching the *Sears Catalog* to see what "real ladies" wore, to striving to discover the meaning of life, love and the universe beyond, welcome to Ruth's eclectic world.

—Jan Tannarome

LIVING AND LEAVING

I give you my love, more precious than money.
I give you myself before preaching.

O public road, I say back, I'm not afraid to leave you, yet,
I love you.

Each house I've loved and not been afraid to leave.

Sixty-plus in all.

The first I remember: a small unfurnished apartment above
Doc Williams' store. It was my first unfurnished home after
Fred Finch, bare and cold. Was I afraid to leave and
did I love it? Too long ago.

Since then, studio apartments, large apartment, small cottages, old
Victorians, tumbledown shacks, dormitories, Quonset huts, project
duplexes, just ordinary houses. Each one I've loved
and not been afraid to leave.

In some I loved the coziness, in others the light. I loved the
oldness or quaintness of others.

Or the gardens of snapdragons, stock, pansies, and marigolds.

The color entertained me in some, and the simplicity soothed
me in others. They were not very grand, yet everywhere
there were stories.

There are endless things I could say about loving and leaving. Maybe
I've been too ready to leave, maybe I've not loved
deeply enough so leaving was not fearful. Yet, perhaps I
instinctively knew that all of life was loving and leaving or perhaps
my early life led me to this conclusion. Now I think I not only love my
house, it is the perfect house for me.
There are lacks to be sure. Not enough wall space for paintings, worn

out floors, a small living room. It is mostly large enough and even yet every room has a stack in it.

Books to be read, collages to be made, pictures to be framed or hung.

Clothes to be folded or given away. Stacks of paper to sift and sort. Piles of poems, short stories, essays.

It is the perfect house; it is large enough, has an office section and a studio section. There are large storage areas. Ample decks to sit on under trees and stars, and creatures to watch—deer, a skunk, a possum and a rattlesnake.

Can I now say I'm not afraid to leave you, yet I love you?
No, I can't—not just now.

AN ORDINARY DAY
September 3, 2018

Once when someone said
Oh, just an ordinary day,
I yawned, prayed never me.
Thought poor soul,
An ordinary day!
I would be embarrassed,
Ashamed, desperate.
Only ordinary people
Have ordinary days.

I don't want to say this
Yet, aloud,
I am not ready yet
To admit,
I'll whisper it.

I long for ordinary days.
I relish ordinary days.
I hope for one
After a string of
Un-ordinary days.
I pray for ordinary days.

Weeping, all I want
Is ordinary days,
When the sun quietly
Climbs the sky
No hello, whistles,

Spectacular event,
Just the sun.

I walk rather than run
As the day moves forward.
The tasks are simple,
Everyday,
A shower, oatmeal with walnuts,
A walk through the woods
Behind the house.
Not a run, a walk
With deep breaths of fresh air
Cleansing my lungs, soul, everything.

Simple everyday tasks,
Dishes washed, bed made,
House put in order
Read the newspaper,
Gaze out the window for five minutes,
Feels like forever.
Time to write
A poem or two.
Maybe an essay or memoir.
Stare off into space at—
Well—nothing.

Lunch,
Simple, quiet
Make a call or two
Then a nap.

Still the most delicious part
Of an ordinary day,
Write poetry,
A short story,
Work on the painting,
Fifteen years,
Very bad painting.
Best of all
It never has to be good.

The afternoon lingers as I reflect,
Most deliciously.
Putter and putter
Until dinner.
Quiet, simple
Maybe a candle
Or a small bouquet
Maybe a dear person
To share wine, good
Conversations.
Maybe all in solitude.

Dark descends, slowly
Twilight becomes night,
Ordinary night.
Closing up the house,
Turning off the lights,
Feeling my way to bed,
One last look.

In bed
Contentment, cats,
Welcome rest,
Gratitude.
An ordinary day.
The presence in the room
Smiles in agreement.
Solitude.

Oh God!
Give me more ordinary days.

CHANGE

When we breathe new air
Drop our old anxieties old concerns

Newness creeps in
Unaware we shift slightly
New taste on our tongue

Cells shift in anticipation
An undetected shudder

Startled we stop, stare together
Bearing our own wildness

We sit, reflect
Under a different sky

EVENING
July 20, 2016

Two birds sitting on the top of the tree,
chatting.
Underneath houses, everywhere
houses.
I wonder did anyone consult
the birds?
I suppose not, weren't we
most important?

CHRISTMAS DAY
January, 2018

༄

Christmas Day—emptiness, quiet, bare streets

Swerving traffic
Dodging back forth
Noise mixed together in a din
Start stop start stop
And fly—fly—honking
Skidding
Sailing as if on sea
Only the freeway.

It stopped one day only.
One day.
Peaceful emptiness,
Silence, quiet.
Listening to the noise
Of silence.
Soothing,
Deepening.
Empty parking lots.
Trashy still, but empty.

Tears fell,
Visions of fields teeming with life,
Grasses—multicolored,
Rich as earth,
Flowers—bright as the sun,
Heat shimmering,
Trees sing to the sun
Rising and setting.
Soft music of scurrying and rattling,
Some mewing.
A different time descending.
Soothing,
Wrapping a body
In warm breezes.
Another time now gone.
Another day brings back
The speedy noisy crashing
Rhythm of now.

ODE TO ANIMALS
May 4, 2018

Stay away from the fence

She yelled

Those colts will trample you

I stayed away from the fence

I watched the black colts play

I did not play

Don't go near the barn

She yells

The bull will gore you

I stayed away from the barn

I watched the bull snort and stamp

I did not snort or stamp

Come in the house this minute

She yells

Those dogs may have rabies and bite you

I came in the house quickly

I watched the dogs yelp and play

I did not yelp and play

Dangerous animals
Danger everywhere
Dangerous life
Thunder and lightning

Dangerous everywhere
Watch out for bugs, birds, snakes, lizards,
cats that scratch,
Dogs that bite, trampling horses, raging bulls
Watch out, watch out

FLYING
May 4, 2018

I saw you fly

But snakes don't fly

You flow in front of me

My jaw dropped and I stopped

Your jaw showed long fangs

And your tail rattled close to my nose

I saw you fly

Or did you leap at me and miss?

I can't imagine it was a miss

Was it a message?

I saw your diamond-shaped head

Curled down toward me

Your eyes were like red coals

You stared hard at me

I wanted to turn away

I wanted to run

I was frozen in place on the path

I remembered you in the morning

I wondered what you wanted

Were you a warning?

Did you want to strike me?
What was your message?

I saw you fly
I was walking on a trail
And there you were
It was a dream I think
I can't imagine it was real
Maybe you are real somewhere in me

But poets don't fly
You flew in front of me
Beckoning to me
I resisted not knowing
You persisted ... damn

You leaped at me
I can't imagine it was a miss
You tried again a different trick
Words stumbling forward
You persisted still!
Damn you!

I saw you fly
Your eyes were coy, inviting
You smiled at me
I shrugged my shoulders
I wanted to leave
You persisted and persisted

I remember you in the morning
Slithering around in my dream
What was your message?
What do you want? I struggled
Oh, are you persistent!

I saw you fly
I was taking a class
And there you were sitting in a chair
It was a dream I think
I can't imagine it was real
Maybe I know you somewhere in me
Poet, where are you?

PEOPLE HERE
May 3, 2018

People here
        Now all gone
And I serenely watch the sky
Brilliant blue, scattered
Heavily with gray and white

A winter tree stark against the blueness
Old against the gray and white

And I am glad for
These quiet moments in my life.
Equally glad for the people, too

        Who are now gone.

FAMILY
January 3, 2018

My brother dying alone—
The wound of his head blown away
Symbol of the wound he lived
The oozing pain—spilled everywhere
An escape—a shot—a fatal wound

My mother—proud, grieving
Containing, hiding her wound,
Burying the pain in a secret place
Encasing with a well-formed crust
A kernel hidden in pride—denial

My father—collapsed in guilt,
Spilling, burying everyone in his path
Wearing the guilt, sinking into it.
Lost in years of enduring grief
Spilling tears, a constant reminder—full of failure

Two brothers left
Sharing their story of grief.
Grieving together, wishing, wanting to help
Helpless in their awareness of destructive pain.

Bound by the story—premature death suffering
A wife, a family in confusion
Bitterness, anger, fear, lashing rage
Reforming, shaping a life, hanging on to the known
Remember reliving years unresolved destroying
A prevailing fear of fragility and what it meams

The sister waiting for the inevitable
Yet hit, knocked cold by the reality.
Angry—sad—the failed helper
Determined to be free of the story
Bound by a story, a struggle, a family

FOOD

Chocolate to soothe me
Coffee to enliven me
Morning pastry to warm me.

Wine to calm me
Cake, pie, cookies to nourish me
Ice cream to remind me
Joys of childhood
Even though they were few.
Bread, French, sourdough
Rye, ancient wheat to sustain me.

Do I ever think of the nutritious value?
Yes of course
Guiltily, shamefully.
Do I eat for the nutritious value?
Importance to my health?
Rarely.
I'm ruled by other needs, desires, callings.

CHATTING WITH TREES
July 20, 2020

I wander from birds to

trees.

I love chatting with

trees.

They are so quiet,

respectful.

Listen so carefully

and nod appropriately.

Yet there is a sadness about

trees.

They, like the birds, have been

so replaced, unconsulted.

And who are we?

THE GYPSY

A gypsy calls to me.
Dances before me, entices me
Dark sultry eyes
Bracelets clinking and clanging, luring me
Long red fingernails
Matching her red sash
Swishing, twirling
Calling to me
Her neckline plunges
Her thin blouse
Revealing bare breasts

Swirling wild skirt
Tapping feet.
Come she says, come
No, I say no
Maybe 20 years ago
Maybe even 10
No, I say no
I watch as she fades away
No longer calling to me.

OPOSSUM
May 4, 2018

I saw you walk along the wire
Your naked tail dragging along
Your manner meek and mild
Walking along the wire

I saw you on the ground
The dog barked, fur rising
You opened your mouth
Exposing sharp little teeth
Snarling and puffed up

The dog barked and moved toward you
Snarling and growling
Suddenly you fell over and lay there
Are you dead? I asked myself
The dog moved over and sniffed at you

Gasping the dog picks you up
Shaking you, holding you in his mouth
Growling and shaking you
Like a rag doll you are limp
Bored, the dog lets go

Running after a new excitement
The dog leaves
Minutes and minutes pass
You lie there as I watch
Finally you waddle off

You always seemed to be walking a tightrope,
a possum on the wire
Dragging nakedness behind you
Oh, your manner meek and mild
A sly quiet possum

You crawled to the ground
Sniffing with your nose
I approached you carefully
You hissed at me
I didn't stop

I barked at you in fury
You snarled behind your smile
Suddenly you fell to the ground
Quietly you lay
I knew you were playing dead

I wanted to poke at you

I wanted to shake you

I spit on you

And left you to lie

WOMAN
January 3, 2018

Woman awakening,

To the dreams, to the soul—

Rising out to light

Images filling the room and

filling the space inwardly and outwardly

MEDITATION
June, 2012

I am the one who
while meditating

My brain slips out of my body
       and travels to the past, the future
          and to fantasize

What might have been
what might be
    some times
somewhere
      and never became real,

but the brain still goes there

hope still hangs there

The next breath
maybe I'll return and
all of me will be there,
    Brain
        Body

and Breath

BEVERLY
September 1, 2012

My life is like a blossoming garden
filled with wonder and color and green growth.

My life is filled to overflowing
with healing light and of being healed.

Poem

I am Beverly
who became
Ruth
who became
earth
who became
space
who became God
who became
Beverly
who became
Ruth
who became earth
who became
space
who became
God
who became
Beverly
who became
Ruth

LIVING
June, 2012

How do any of us decide to live?

For dying is no worse—no better than living—both just are.

There can be no judgment of the value of either.

And I have decided to live.
        To watch the sunrise and sunset.

To hear birds sing, cry and warn each other.
        To look at squirrels in the fall gathering together.

And green leaves in spring, gold and yellow ones in the fall.
        To love and be loved and know I'm wanted.
        To be open about the parts of me that rarely show.

Oh, well, what a little fun will do for the soul.

Not take ourselves so seriously.

Be at peace and enjoy.

There is joy in living.

There is peace in my heart and my soul is smiling.

We are free together.

Secure in me to take a risk of exposure.

Changing from day to day.

It's love of flowers, humanness, birds and animals.

It's love for me.

Be aware right now. Don't wait for tomorrow. Be aware now.

WHEN I PLAN
January 3, 2018

When I plan, I write not!

Two friends met and joined together for a lifetime.

They met in an eternity, joined together as seeds, grew,
    were born, flourished in life, nurtured one another.

The pain of one became the pain of the other.
Neither felt separately, but in their closeness
    whatever one was so was the other.

The beauty of one enhanaced the beauty of the other.
The ugliness of one became the pain of the other.

Together they grew old, tired and worn.
Together they died, to leave one another for another eternity.

One turned to dust and water.
The other went back to the air and the fire.

And the friends joined so tightly together in this life
    now are separate.

For the soul no longer needs the body
As the body no longer can house the soul.

POLARITY
January 3, 2018

Is everything a polarity?

It seems so

The words will come

Life goes and none of us know where

Caught in its stream

We flow, rage, bounce, get caught, spin,
and our travels are not our dreams.

It is our life and its route unknown, uncharted

To be more serious than I like

To be less beautiful than I want

To be wiser than I know

To be poorer and care less

To lead and heal—none of this I dreamt—but it is here

To be alone longer than life. This is me

To be plumper than is glamorous

To be not lovable, but loved.

To accept what is and still not know!

THE END OF THE OLD

The earth dried up and hardened.
Chemical intervention, a quick fix, and hurry please,
was required.

BUT THE NOURISHMENT OF THE EARTH WAS GOING
GOING GONE!

Lungs filled with pollution thickened and darkened,
Intervention without inconvenience, please, was required.

BUT THE NOURISHMENT OF THE AIR WAS GOING
GOING GONE!

Blood turned to poison in veins dried up and hardened.
A killer loose, radical intervention was required.

The water turned to poison dried up and hardened.
Intervention, not too costly, please, was required.

BUT THE NOURISHMENT OF WATER WAS GOING
GOING GONE!

Skin deceased, shriveled, dried up and hardened.
Radical, chemical, surgical intervention was required.

Protection thinned beyond repair, the sun burned and hardened.
But what intervention was required?

NOURISHMENT FROM ALL SOURCES GOING GOING GONE!

Immune systems ceased to function, dried up and hardened.
Rest, nourishment, simplicity were the required intervention.

The earth weakened, unable to recover dried up and hardened.
Rest, nourishment, and simplicity were required.

EVERYTHING WAS GOING, GOING, GONE!
NOURISHMENT FROM ALL SOURCES GOING, GOING, GONE!

Immune systems ceased to function, dried up and hardened.
Rest, nourishment, and simplicity are required.

The earth weakened, unable to recover, dried up and hardened.
Rest, nourishment, and simplicity are required.

EVERYTHING GOING. GONE.
WE ARE A MIRROR TO CREATION
AND
CREATION IS A MIRROR TO US.

BLAME AND HEALING

We all blame, blame, and blame.

The oppressed blame the oppressors.
The oppressor says, "It's my duty."

We all blame, blame, and blame.

The oppressed blame the oppressor.
The oppressors say, "It is your fault."

And the trees turn black and withered.
The water turned murky, slimy, and poisonous.
The sun turned blood-red.
The air became thick and dead.

Men, women and children, young and old, blamed.
Black, red, yellow and white, they blamed.
The rich blamed the poor, the poor blamed the rich.
The Jew, the Pagan, the Buddhist,
  the Christian all blamed someone.
People of the west, the south, the east,
and the north blamed each other.

Everyone blamed and blamed.
We all blamed and blamed.

The oppressor blamed the oppressed.
The oppressor said, "It was only right."

And the trees turned black and withered.
The water turned murky, slimy, and poisonous.
The sun turned blood-red.
The air became thick and dead.

The oppressed looked around and were shocked.
The oppressor looked around and was aghast!

They had forgotten to look.
They had forgotten to see.

The black withered trees,
The murky, slimy, poisonous water,
The blood-red sun,
The thick dead air.

Men, women, and children, young and old, they saw.
Black, red, yellow, and white, they saw.
The rich and the poor, they saw.
The Jews, the Pagans, the Buddhists and the Christians,
    they saw.
The people of the west, south, east, and north, they saw.

They saw the Earth and what they had done.
They began to weep and weep.

They saw the Earth and what they had done.
They saw each other.
And they worked, prayed together and played together.
As they cleaned up the Earth.
As they nourished the Earth.
As they loved and cared for the Earth.
As they loved and cared for each other.

And the Earth began to heal.
And the people and all creatures began to heal.

MYSTERY
2020

Where have the nouns gone?
Maybe it is a secret.
Have you noticed?
The nouns are disappearing!

Sometimes they sneakily reappear,
When I least expect them.
When I am doing something important.
Sometimes real important.

Where do they go?
Into the deep recesses of the brain,
Dark corner somewhere?
Only to sneak out,
When least expected.

Or jumping out, at odd
Unexpected times.
Disappearing all together,
Never to return.

I notice there are fewer of them.
Sometimes I never find them.
I may find them later, happily.
Two seconds, they are gone again.
Abandoning me.

I wonder ... do they have the upper hand?
Torturing us relentlessly,
Slippery, hiding, watching.
Sneaking in and out.

RIVER WATER
November 26, 2002

River water running deep and dark

Sparkled with light here and there

Deepened with darkness

Running swiftly and loudly to the deeper water

Pools slow and murky, deep and dark

Sitting stagnant, gathering moss

Like my soul, like my deeper self, the river water runs, sits, gathers light and darkness.

Yet, I want often for only light, pushing hard
on the darkness,
sometimes letting go and seeing my reflection
in the darkness and my dancing in the light.
River water of the soul.

Taking time to be with myself. Hear who I am
and not wonder so much about others.
I can barely write.
I so much just want to sit.
My head hurts and it's finally subsiding.
I hope the move gives me time for a while to really sit,
enjoy a cup of coffee and reflect.

BIRDS ON FIRE

Eagles aflame soaring across the sky,
Leaving a trail of smoke,
A streak of fire
Searing the blueness
Disappearing into the Universe
Invisible–gone, transformed

Birds on fire
Blackened by the smoke
Charred by the flame
Spiraling into specks against the blue
Smaller–smaller–disappearing–gone, transformed

Birds on fire
Agitated dancing among the flames
Turning to smoke wisping away
Trailing into the clouds against the blueness
Thinner–thinner–disappearing, invisible, transformed

Birds on fire
Shaking their feathers
Stamping on the flames glow spread
Leap and scream into the Universe
Stark bright against the blueness
Exploding–gone, invisible, transformed

OAXACA
Mexico, May 4, 2018

Christo on the cross
Overlooks Oaxaca
    His nose twitches
Fillled with odors
    Stale beer
    Wine breath
    A little shit, a little urine
Old fumes, exhausts
    Mixed with hot odors
    Baking bread
    Spices sweet, sour, strong

The Virgin sits on the church steeple
    Her greedy eyes frozen stare
Spiked red heels
Undulating hips, luring lips
    Waning color
    Houses, fake flowers, plastic balloons
    Too much to see
Shriveled old ladies
    Naked singing children
    Brown and pale

The angel soars carrying a trumpet
Flies over the square
 Ears are filled
 Honking, singing horn
 Off key songs guitars
 Crashing here
 Pounding
 Hawking voices filled with wares
She drops her trumpet
The good news beat her here

Under the cross, the steeple
 And the flying angel
 Me tasting strong new flavors
 Moved by the sweeping brush
 Taken by the song
 Burned by the colors
 Caught in the din

Rise to Christo
Sit with the Virgin
Fly with the angel
Over Oaxaca.

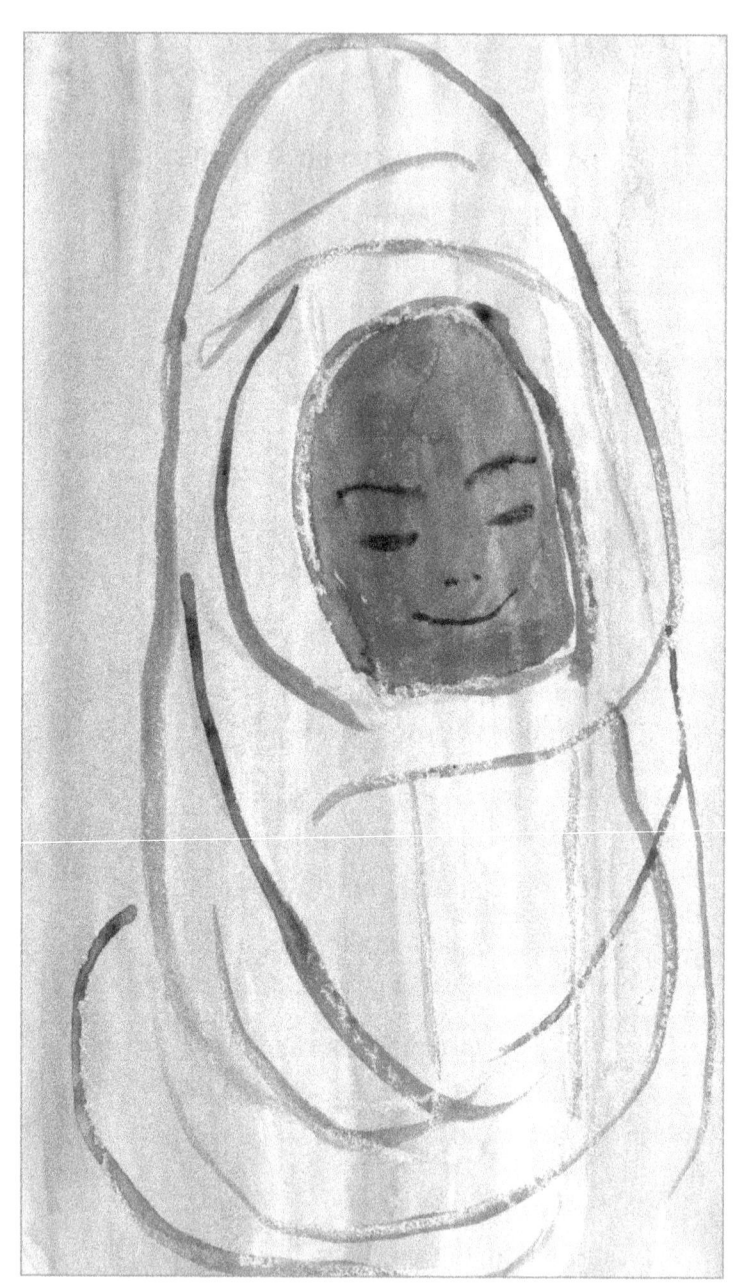

REVEALING

Revealing an abortion or two

The secret suicide

The bastard birth

Mixed marriage

Lesbian relationships

The shotgun wedding

A member of a strange religion

Masturbating and choking sounds

Fantasy and shame

The guarded affair

The deceitful failure

When I was crazy

Anorexia

CAKE MAKING—CONTACT PAPER—ALCOHOL IN MY FAMILY

Where are you Spirit?
I thought I had found you
In this holy sacred place.
This mountain
This ancient ruin
This beautiful building
This holy person.
I have felt you in all these places
I had to stay or go to these places
Regularly, often, reverently
I wanted you with me in me
I thought I found you
    In daily sitting
    Hands open,
    Legs crossed
    Remembering my breath
    Chanting to the gods
I felt you in those times
I had to pray light candles sit
Regularly often reverently
I wanted you in me with me
They say you are everywhere
And yet nowhere.
After many years Spirit
I felt you in the trees
Surrounding my home

In the birds at the fountain or
Scrambling for a place at the feeder
Looking at the night sky and
      in breathing
That seemed simple of course
      you were in the creation of things
One day on the treadmill
In the gym watching television
Watching as all the world
Could become an execution
I cried and I felt creation cry with me.
Some thought I was strange
Few knew what I was saying
Often now I cry with God
      through 9/11 through Katrina through Southeast Africa
      during the war, each war
Afghanistan, Iraq, and the next one and the one after that.
I feel God's tears as the air is unbreathable,
      the soil grows nothing, the water is thick with toxins,
      and I wear a beautiful red silk jacket from China.
But when I saw you in a chair
Felt you in the cup I held
Experienced your presence in the table where I sat
I had a sense of everything and yet nothing.
If the chair was smashed the cup broken,
      the table collapsed

Spirit you are here.
  In meanness, in kindness
  In violence, in gentleness
  In suffering and peace
You are present.
  I wanted it different
  It is not
  I wanted Spirit just in love and goodness
   in peace.
  There is nothing I can do to change
   all the manifestations
   around me
I can with thought care and respect
look more deeply inward and transform myself
  only myself
  and
   offer myself.

POEM FOR NINA
April 9, 2018

When the wind blows so hard you can hardly walk,
tatters your clothes and mats your hair,
fills it with leaves and twigs,
Dust stings you as it hits your body
Finally you just sit down, and let it blow.

The cold hard demanding rain begins to fall.
You are soaked.
Quietly the rain softens, warm, gentle, relaxing. Your tears join
the falling rain.

You look up into green leaves,
Blooming dogwood, redbud, cherry trees,
Notice the beauty of the earth, the daffodils,
Daisies, orange poppies, wild violets.
And you sigh and sigh, the tears roll.

Finally you rise, walk into your home, dress,
Knowing in your heart the wind may come again
Wishing it wouldn't.
Even knowing, you still hope
The wind is done with you.
And it probably isn't.

PUT BACK 'TIL NEXT TIME
April 30, 2018

They laid babies on
their backs,
As they now do again.
I have images
Do I have feelings?
I don't know
Can I be the baby again?

Lying on my back
In a metal crib
the world appears as horizontal
stripes and nothing else.

It is always the same
Change diapers
Pick up
Put bottle in mouth
sucking, feeding
Done
Put back
'Til next time

I remember it even now
Always on time a rhythm
6-8-10-12-2-4
Nothing changes
6-Change diapers,
pick up–hold–feed
Put back.

10-12-2-4-6 Again, again, again
March of time
March hour by hour
Always on time, a rhythm
Something changes.
A new rhythm
6-10-2-6-10-2

Now there are two worlds.
One with horizontal stripes
The other world where
Some smile some just get the job done
Some babble at me
I watch and watch and watch

No need to cry
Everything taken care of
No need to cry
Never hungry for long
Never wet for long.
Never messy for long.

I want to cry
I do cry
Doesn't make a difference
Nothing changes.

6-10-2-6-10-2
Change diapers
Pick up hold
Put a bottle in my mouth.
Sucking feeding
Put back
Disappears
6-10-2
I love routine.

RALPH
September 4, 2012

I want to remember my brother's yellow eyes.

I want to remember the one dimple in his left cheek.

I want to remember when suddenly he went
from 5'2" to 5'10" the year
      he was 18.

I want to remember him in his uniform
when I tried to teach him to
      dance.

I want to remember how he studied in college
to become an engineer.

I want to remember how hard he tried.

Now to remember I dream I never saw the pain
in his yellow eyes.

Now to remember I dream I saw him smile and laugh
      more than he ever did.

Now to remember I dream of the man he never was
even though he was
      finally 5'10" and died at the age of 49.

Now to remember I dream we never had that last fight
      before he died.

Now to remember I dream he had stayed Baby Boy
and had not tried so
      hard and failed so much.

Now to remember I dream he is an old man 15 months
younger than I
      playing golf with my other two brothers.

I GIVE YOU MY LOVE
May 3, 2018

I give you love more than money.

Who are you that say love me, come with me

Forget security

Forget safety

How

I give you my love more precious than money.

Who are you that offer love?

Do you offer security, safety, warm hearth, winter hats beautiful jewelry?

Tell me how will you pay for the furnace?

Who are you that give love more precious than money?

I give you myself before preaching or law.

Who are you that offer yourself?

Do you offer comfort, peace, soothing times, no chaos?

Tell me how well you know how to judge accurately the situation.

    (And be morally right?)

Who are you that give self before preaching or law?

You ask to give myself

To what? I ask.

Fear, discomfort, insecurity, confusion, chaos, turmoil.

They are all too familiar too old in me to give myself to them

You ask to give myself

Come travel with you?

Where? How? I ask.

Destinations unknown

Unfamiliar place, strange

    beds, stranger food, stranger persons.

They are all too frightening to beg for my small person.

Come travel

    with you?

Who is it that asks so much of me and yet so little?

My soul's yearning.

JUNE
May 3, 2018

She taught me to cheat at cards

I was naive

June, my brother's wife

She must be really good in bed

Why else, why else does he put up with her?

June growing up in Los Molinos

She's a liar Marilyn said

I hated her and she always lied

Marilyn never had anything good to say

June out for a night dancing drinking

She lied to the rodeo cowboy

He claimed he didn't have a wife in Wyoming

I'm Ruth Ghio, she declared

And she danced to the Tennessee Waltz

In a Mineral bar drinking, dancing, lying

June denying the lie with a lie and another lie

It must have been Marilyn she claimed

And the lie slid across the barroom floor

It must have been Marilyn

And the lie crawled down the street

I don't believe you and the lie floated over the mountain

It landed on my doorstep

It must have been Marilyn she claimed

June married my ex-husband

And the lie slipped forever into my life

June re-married my brother

And the lie continues forever in my life

I was naive

I really did want to believe she was a liar, so I nodded my head,
   but still
      hoping it was the truth

My father's comment, "She must be really good in bed."

I was taken back

I knew how to cheat at cards, but she was better at it than me

I was too scared of my dark side

I enjoyed hers

Rodeo cowboy local rancher

Wife he left in Wyoming

SELF-LOVE
October 15, 2018

Self Love is one weedy stalk
one weedy stalk
shrunken bending over
leafless—just one weedy stalk

Does it live in the heart
or somewhere between the ribs and the spine
I can feel it in my loneliness
as it searches for a response

I can tell how alive it is by how it feels me or not
mostly not
I protect it hiding way back behind my eyes

The slits are dark and shaded
The eyes somewhere far back,
watching for danger
carefully building a protective wall

brick by brick saving it
wanting it a hollow place in my body
my chest clenches stomach sickens
breathing harsh pulled back

I sit on the floor sob deep hiccup sobs
looking for the twig saving it
as meager as it is
determined to love

the arms surround it
heart beats to keep alive
breath blows life slowly
deeply blows life slowly
deeply and the twig is there

"... that self-love is the one weedy stalk ..."
from: *Faint Music* by Robert Hass

WELCOME

When the mother looked down on her babe,
new to her arms,
Did she imagine her as girl
Filled with energy, exploring the world,
dreaming of far away places?

Did she notice her baby's richness?
Like the light golden richness of spring.
The sweet fiery nature of the girl in her arms, her depth
her capacity for healing.

In her arms she felt her baby snuggle,
smile with the contact.
Did she notice the multitude of expressions?
Sadness, grief, to joy and delight?

Did she imagine the baby in her arms
as a healer?
Sensing her gentleness, her kindness, her empathy.
Did she smile, sensing the specialness of the newborn she held,
gazing at her deeply?

Hello, Ginger, welcome to the world.
I know you will live well.
It won't always be easy.
And as I look at you,
I know you will be OK.
My lovely baby girl, Ginger.

TODAY
May 3, 2018

Today I read what I wrote

I wish I hadn't

I don't like it

Nor the part of me it reflects.

I want to destroy what is written

I want to cling to what is written

And I let it lie

Never wanting to share it again.

Now it seems needful, infantile, and stupid.

Is that true?

I don't know

It just feels that way today.

I-80
May 4, 2018

Driving down I-80
Unpacking
Laughing
Eating and drinking
Sleeping
Talking

Driving down I-80
Filled with thought, ideas
Distracted by light after light
Traffic thickened and thinned
Wrong lane, wrong turn
Correction before too late

Driving down the dark I-80 freeway
My mind filled with strange thought and ideas
   about myself, the world
Distracted by the lights from opposing traffic
   stringing together in a long line
The traffic thickened, a long stream
   and thinned to a trickle
I'm in the wrong lane and must turn in to the school
A safe correction, the wrong turn unnecessary
Finally a safe arrival

Here I am
Driving down the dark I-80 freeway watching drips
   of rain fall,
        hearing the roar

Here I am
My mind rattling filled with strange thoughts,
   ideas and visions about myself
        the world

Here I am
Distracted by the glaring lights from opposing
   traffic, tightening,
        holding my breath

Here I am
The traffic thickened to a long stream and thinned
   to a trickle
I smelled the smoke, grease and oil thicken and thin

Here I am
I'm scanning the road and still make a wrong
   turn into the
        overwhelming school

Here I am
A safe correction, a sigh of relief
The wrong turn unnecessary
I feel my breath again
Here I am
Finally the quiet street, the arbor of trees comes
   into my sight a
        safe arrival

MY CHILDREN
May 3, 2018

I look at my eldest, not one of my birth children,

Tall, bony clear-skinned and clear-eyed

Even in appearance.

And I see her anger and hatred buried deep for me amongst her despair.

And I trust

For I have walked that road before and I have learned

Understanding—acceptance and loving care.

I look at my next child.

My first born—a daughter

Tall and dark, brown hair, brown eyes and dark skin,

All touched by earth.

And I see her hurt, her young ideals and rebellion riding high

And I trust

For I have walked that road also and I have learned

Patience, faith and strength to accept what is and what may never be.

I look at my third child. A daughter also.

Small-boned graceful touched by beauty

From God knows where.

And I see her loneliness, her sadness and her fear.

Bricks piled high and challenging the world.

And I trust

For I too have been there and learned

To be creative, the necessity of sharing, and welcoming the world.

I look at my youngest child.

A son born into a female world.

Tall, brown flowing hair and sensitive eyes often filled with fear.

And I see his keen awareness, sensitive perception
   often used against himself.

And I trust

For again, I have walked that road before

I have learned to trust myself, and wonder at the world
   and live bravely

Each day.

Each a part of me. And I a part of them.

Learning together and from each other.

TO FEEL A BODY'S WARMTH
May 3, 2018

To feel a body's warmth next to mine
To touch gently, caressingly
To feel the pulsating beat of another life.

To touch the breath of one near.
To feel the moisture of a kiss
And see frank desire in another's eyes
To smell the odor of a man's closeness.

To want, to need deeply internally
These are the things I think of when thoughts of you
Enter my being.

I don't revisit this desire or longing often any more.
And when I do the same thought, feelings and desire
Rise up in me. Now some forty years later.

I can still imagine a body's warmth next to mine
And be engulfed by this heat.
To touch gently softly caressingly the other's skin
encouraging a tingling within.

To feel the pulsating beat of other life.
Is freeing the rhythm—relieving the strife.
To touch the breath of one near
Is being sensitized aware of one held dear.

To feel the first hot moisture of a kiss
Gives ache to all I now miss.
To see frank desire in one's eyes
And respond in kind—no fear
No lies.

To smell the odor of a man's nearness.
Desiring—wanting—hungry—needing

These thoughts
    Concerning you
        Reach the depth of my being.

MAYBE IT'S TIME

Maybe it's time for a cabin on the beach
To hang up my hat.

To read all those books gathering dust on my shelves
To leave this life behind.

Maybe it's time to draw those pictures, throw those pots
Not see the troubled faces.

For long walks by the ocean, sitting rocks, gazing places
To listen only to the waves.

Maybe it's time for a simple life, quiet, solitude
Not to witness another's pain.

To write my stories, my poetry, my novel and other little ditties
No more reports, progress notes, ethical issues.

How will I do it?

Maybe it's time to carry my fear in my hand
As I've certainly told others.

To jump off the cliff, to fly, to soar, or risk the crash
I have so often encouraged others to do.

TRAPPED
September 12, 2012

My mind is full and blank at the same time.

Yesterday I was a daughter
Today I'm a mother
Yesterday and today now one
Puzzling over how to relate
Confused, puzzled, curious—
How do I make contact with them.
Rejecting—rejected continuous into space.
Unresolved, struggled trapped.

Well yesterday I was a daughter
Puzzling over how to relate to my mother
      Curious, puzzled, confused.
      Knowing rejection—not wanting to reject, but
      unresolved, struggled, trapped.

Now, today I am a mother
      Struggling to be with a daughter.
      Confused, wanting to be understood
      Desperate in my efforts to be heard.

And to hear—
      Knowing rejection—not wanting to reject, but
      Unresolved struggle, trapped.

Sandwiched in the middle
Caught with their definition of me.
But old—no longer true, but yet true.

Maybe it's time to be wild, to be free, to live for me.
Yet I have worked so hard to belong here.

Before I die, to touch the earth to live all my dreams
Before I die is it possible?

Maybe it's time to let go as they say
to leave, to live, to die.

"My daughter," she says.
"My mother," she says.
"My mother," I say.
"My daughter," I say.

Looking both ways at once.
"Trapped—the middle one"—I say.
Still a mother.
Still a daughter.
Neither knowing me—nor me them.
Person—woman—human.

A photograph colored by their need to define me—
    and my need to
        define them.

How I need them to be.
How they need me to be.

Identity linked, defined, shaped.
Connected—a chain binding each
generation to the next—unbreakable.

    Trapped by the daughter
    Trapped by the mother
    Both of whom are me.

BLACK CAT

Climbing out of bed
Turning on the heat
Feeding the cat
Turning off the alarm
Looking out the door
Meditating first

Feeding the cat, yawning, scratching my head
Finding the food, pouring it into her dish
Running down the stairs, stopping
Looking away, not interested
Waits for me to leave
Poor black neurotic little creature

Feeding the black little cat
Yawning, scratching my head
Finding her special food, pouring it into her dish
Running down the stairs, a black whirl
Then stopping, watching
Looking away from me disdainful, pretending not to be interested
Watching and waiting for me to look down
    and leave
Poor black neurotic little creature waits for me
    to disappear, then eats

The beginning day

Noticing the morning light

Feeding the little black cat

I yawn quietly, scratch my head

The beginning day

Finding her special food hidden in a cupboard

Pouring her food into her special blue dish, noticing the pet food smell

The beginning day

Running down the stairs, a black furry whirl

Stopping fast, then carefully watching me

The beginning day

Looking away I observe her disdain, pretending disinterest

I watch curiously

The beginning day

Watching intensely, waiting for me to leave, not moving a muscle

I'll wait too

The beginning day

Pure black anxious tense little creature
   waits for me to disappear

I hear the crunch

MY SON

When my son and I talked about my death

When the rocking chair creaked

When my son cried

When I cried

When he assumed responsibility

When I knew I was loved

When my sensitive loving son and I talked about my unknown death

When the old cane rocking chair creaked

When my dear son sobbed and cried

When I chokingly cried

When he assumed the burdensome responsibility

When I knew I was deeply loved

The old rocking chair creaked

The quiet was filled with noiseless sound

My son cried

The old rocking chair creaked

The quiet was filled with noiseless sound

We talked quietly about my dying

The old rocking chair creaked

The quiet was filled with noiseless sound

I sobbed

The old rocking chair creaked

The quiet was filled with noiseless sound

He agreed to the task

The old rocking chair creaked

The quiet was filled with noiseless sound

I knew I was loved

The old rocking chair creaked

The quiet was filled with noiseless sound

BINGO
May 3, 2018

The old ones are all here—
Gathered together, their cards
Under their arms—
Feet shuffling along
Slowly hunched over peering
Over glasses—eyeing the room
Holding hard to purses
Leaning on canes
Pushing their walkers
Smiling greeting each other
Melding together
"Hello did you walk?" she asks.
"No, Joe brought me."
Most come alone, a few with spouses,
Fewer yet bring a guest
"Oh this is my niece."
Shaking hands, nodding
"Glad to meet you."

"Where are you sitting?"
"In the non-smoking."
"Good we will join you,"
To me, her guest

"Here you sit here.
I will show you how."
"Well good luck."
"Thank you, you too."
"They will start soon."
Another conversation, unemotional
Stark, matter of fact
"How's your daughter?"
"Fine, she survived surgery.
She will be home soon."
"Did they get it all?"
"Don't know yet."
Resignation, blended with hope
Fear hidden in the small talk
Acceptance creeping along the edges
Examines the room, slides her chair back.
Nodding, "Cancer—chemotherapy."
"All that stuff"
"I am going over to talk to her."

Awareness of a room
Of the old ones
On a Saturday night out.

The game begins, everyone prepares
Equipment out—card holders—large marking pens.
New games—Double Bingo,
Postage Stamp, 7 Pack, Lazy L, Crazy T, Layer Cake
Intensity—hope waiting
Watching marking clicking away
Bingo rings through the air.

Losers groan, until the next round.
Voices calling numbers
Lights light up the board!
Anticipation only one number here
two numbers here
Watching all five cards
A distant bingo.
The evening proceeds, smoke fills the room
Burns eyes noses chests
Finally the last game
Last hope, last chance maybe a win!
No luck—going home,
Shuffling out the old ones—
Picking up equipment
Bent over stiff from hours of sitting,

Holding purses tightly clenched to the shapeless body.
Leaning on canes, pushing walkers
Shuffling out slowly, even when moving fast
Moving to the door together
Saying "Goodbye" going home.
Lonely houses, quiet houses, TV sets
Long nights, days filled with activities.
Staying alive, finding pleasure simply each day.

AFTER BINGO
August 26, 2012

Long nights days filled with activities.
Coffee at Walkers,
greeting friends in the morning
Watching TV going for a walk
Buying groceries, watching TV
President of the Women's Club
31 on Wednesdays, card game with friends
Current Affairs Class on Tuesday.
Exercise, watching TV
Family and friends sometimes gather
in her old living room,
unchanged in 30-plus years.
Too tired to travel—too nervous to drive.
The day-to-day business of living
Slow tedious tasks.

GIFTS
May 4, 2018

I give you books

You give me a 30-year-old ring

Made of turquoise from the Iroquois tribe

Dusty, musty precious books

Filled with words, stories, images

I loved and still love

An elegant beautiful simple ring

Touched by your generosity

Moved by the love I feel for you

From you

I sit here stuck tongue-tied

Worried, slightly embarassed

Do you know how precious to me the books are?

I know about the ring and its meaning

Spiritual, magical your connection to your people

I will cherish the ring certainly

Can I possibly share with you the meaning of books?

The places they have taken me into myself, my thoughts, my feelings

Into the souls of others

I will cherish the ring

Not because of the ring

But because of who we are to each other

And then the words, expansive, lyrical

Filled with meaning

The meaning I have given them
I give you empathy
You give me beauty
    A gift of beauty
    This ring
    Turquoise stone set in silver
    Hand-braided
    Hand polished
Books as gifts of empathy
To touch your heart
To open to your own softness
We weep together
    My gift of empathy
    Pours out of your gift of beauty
    Together they are more
I will look at my hand
I will smile and remember you
I will see you in the beautiful silver turquoise ring
And I wlll see the Iroquois
Also beautiful
    Is this a fair exchange?
    Your gift of beauty
    And mine of empathy?
    Does it matter?
I wonder, do you know

My gift is about empathy

My hope is my heart

My sorrow and grief

> It is hard not to see the beauty
>
> The ring is truly a gift of physical beauty
>
> Emotional beauty, filled with your beauty
>
> And spiritual meaning

The books are to ease your pain

Open you to grief

And let your sorrow pour

Into my hand

I will hold it for you

> I am opened and tenderized by
>
> The beauty and meaning of your gift
>
> A beauty that is much more than the ring
>
> A beauty I see in you

And my empathy is deepened

Your beauty enhanced

The ring may be lost

The books may fall into dust

But between us always

There will be beauty and empathy

OCEAN
May 3, 2018

Part of this is lost
Never to return!
And I feel the loss

Joyful to watch
Sadness too
What was today?
Will it ever return?

Joy for the new
Sadness for the lost and gone
Timeless, endless like the
Human soul.

Brighter, more glistening
More real than ever before.

Crashing noisy violent erupting
To calm peace quiet
Only to begin again—high and violent
Against the rocks.
Soft and peaceful against the sand.

Timeless endless like the human soul.

CODA AND QUINTA
October 3, 2018

Coda, a boxer
proud, determined.

Once young and vibrant,
loved to run, jump, and hit
out with his paws.
The breed is boxer.

He and Quinta, a brindle boxer,
played, fought and ran together,
snapped at each other, barked and growled.
She had her tail docked, he did not.
Neither had the perky standup ears.

Now she is gone
The disease of boxers,
Skin cancer slowed her down.
Dementia changed her.
Finally too much cancer,
they bid her goodbye.

Now Coda has the wrinkled
gray face of the old
sleeps more and more.
Is stone deaf. As I pet him I wonder—
In his dreams does he remember Quinta?
Does he feel the freedom of running,
his pride, his strength?

Does he visit Quinta whose face was
always filled with expression?
Sometimes love, occasionally annoyance,
Frustrated patience and sometimes just disgust.

TREE
2015

I
Twig
sticking in charred earth
lonely bare slanting slightly
surrounded by other twigs
newly pushed into the ground,
for miles and miles.

II
Sapling
skinny branches bare nubs
forking out along the twig
soft breeze leaf buds moving
drooping from drops of rain bowing
in unison song.

III
Tree
Forked branches spreading
hugging the ground a lacy shadow.
The first spring new leaves
miles and miles of little trees
softly a breeze dancing.

IV
Changing
Taller than me, still skinny
roots spread hugging the Earth
shadow now spread out
patterns in the sky, on the earth
a canopy of green.

V
Forest
Tall lean pines, cedar, spruce
appearing above oak leaves
elm, a few maples. A forest
on the edge between valley
and foothill.

VI
Changing
In the fall leaves, orange
to purple appear. Above
green spires pierce the sky. Appear
like dancing ladies,
skirts of brightly colored leaves.

VII
Limbs
Pine needles wave
Among them the cones
Below stark branches dark spindly
against the towering green
the crack of ice is heard.

VIII
Winter
Softly snow fell deep silence
not only heard, but felt.
Sometimes the soft crunch
of animal paws broke
the deep quiet of earth.

IX
Ice slowly melted dripped
the ground now slushy.
The air warm, welcoming
announcing the new season
the next round of life.

X
Now the trees fill the land
As far as an eye could travel trees stood.
Some new buds new leaves
The tall stately ones
always green.

JOY

I can touch your sorrow
For I have known sorrow

I can touch your hurt
For I have known hurt

I can touch your anger
For I have known anger

I can touch your giving
For I have known giving

I cannot touch your love
For I have known so little

I cannot touch your receiving
For I cannot receive

I can touch your fear
For I have known fear

I cannot touch your joy
For I have not known joy

And I feel sorrow, hurt, fear and anger
Most

For the little love—
The little receiving I allow

And for the joy I have never known

CLAY
Port Orford, Oregon, April, 2018

Cliff where the little town overlooking the wide Pacific Ocean.
A girl standing on the cliff awed
Knocked to the ground by the amazing sight. Familiar in one way,
Moving like the prairie grass.
Prairie grass, golden, pale yellow, reddish brown and beige
From where she came.

A risk on a sunny day, after school, walking over the rocks
Half sliding, half running out of control down the cliff.
She walked and walked
Until something gray, wet and glistening caught her eye.
Cautiously she touched it
Carefully she scooped it up and held a lump like a prayer.

She shaped it, rolled it in her hand,
Until she held a bowl. She gazed and gazed
Overcome, the tears rolled the laughter pealed.
Delight as she held it in her hand high giving it to
the ocean. Gratitude
Unfamiliar word.

Home was no longer the chaotic house.
Filled with too many people.
Four to the bed, three brothers and her
Tightly arranged across the wide bed.

Never enough food, money; ragged clothes,
Sometimes held together with a safety pin.
Shoes after a week or two got new cardboard soles.
Replaced every day.
The little alcove hidden under a jutting edge of the cliff,
Facing the awesome water called Ocean
She now called home.

There she forgot the violence when she made the four-legged
animal of no description.
Serenity filled her with each simple bowl
She pinched, smoothed, decorated. Each one different.
Each one hers.
She escaped the chaos in the roar of the ocean.

The solitude she craved surrounded her, filled her.
A silence deeper than the ocean roar
A contentment she had never known.
Every afternoon around four o'clock
she entered the house, announcing,
"I stayed after school to help the teacher." No one
doubted her or questioned her.

Each day she returned, to find her current collection of bowls,
animals and people changed,
New forms new shapes all blended together with the sand.
Satisfied she examined how the wind and rain and

the splashes changed their shapes, not destroying them,
just changing them.
She smiled satisfied.

On one late afternoon a voice called her name.
She turned shocked and scared.
"Come home, your mother needs you."
Indeed she did, bruised, black and blue.
She felt a cloak wrap around so tightly
she was grasping for breath.
She wears it still, more loosely,
sometimes it accidently falls off.
More importantly she knows she can take it off
when she feels safe and pulls it tight when she does not.

She called the place on the ocean
(and still does these many years later)
"the clay field,"
the first place she found home,
A real home no one could take from her.
A home that now lives in her
forever and ever.

THE COUPLE

He was an Italian boy just home from the Army.
Notice I said boy, not man,
even though he was after all twenty-two
He was a simple person, easygoing, not demanding.

She was not a girl and she was not a woman
For someone who was practically born
an adult
Of course an adultified child
She was complicated.

They met in his brother's drugstore.
He worked there.
She lived in a fifty-buck-a-month studio apartment
In the old building across the street.
They began to hang out together.
He did not pursue her.
She more than pursued him!

She had many fears laid in her lap
By the culture that informed her about all things.
What if no one wanted her?
And she never married!
After all she was damaged goods.
She had plenty of sex.
When the first man dumped her,
She had thought,
"What's the use?"

Until her second horrible abortion
She had kept a sliver of hope.
Maybe she was wrong.
The first one was in the middle of the night.
Driving to the office blindfolded.

Her friend warning her
Do not look at the doctor.
A dark room, the only light between her legs.

The second one was legal, not because it was legal.
But with just cause, and three doctors agreeing,
And all the papers were signed.
Proving she would be mentally unfit to raise a child.
Even to survive an abortion was iffy,
in regard to her mental health.

She didn't even care.
She went home to a small town up north.
Until getting out of her friend's car,
leaving bloody smears behind her.
The doctor was called.
Another lie to her parents, a rush trip to
The city down south.

A small piece of the placenta, refusing to let go.
The doctor was relieved she had come.
If she had waited, certainly she would have died.
She seriously considered the option.
Another possibility in her life.

Now she was afraid she was a whore.
A loose woman, not a virgin.
Her mind filled with words and images
of skimpy dresses, high heels, walking the streets.
She was sure she would never get married.
She could not imagine being a well-kept mistress
or a high class prostitute.
It was beyond her experience of who she was.
There was no time to grieve; that would come later.

And there he was working in his brother's drugstore.
Freshly home from the Army.
Ripe for the picking.
She didn't even have to bat her eyelashes much
or swish her hips.
Her last hope.

He was an Italian boy just home from the Army.
Notice I said boy,
not man, even though he was after all twenty-two.
He was a simple person, easygoing, not demanding.
A good boy!

She was not a girl and she was not a woman
For someone who was practically born
an adult?
Of course an adultified child
She was complicated.

They were married in Reno.
Sitting on a log by Lake Tahoe she looked up at him.
Oh! My God! What have I done?
She knew the answer: "Saving herself."
A baby girl was born about seven months later.
She came early, you know.
Also came the grief.

She wept when finally Roe v. Wade legalized abortion.
She wept for the children she never bore.
She wept for herself, what she had to do to save her own life.
She prayed that never again,
never again would any woman or girl
go through the fear, the self-loathing and the deep grief.
Covering the shame of not being acceptable,
not being good enough
of being ignorant and stupid.
Oh, yes, of course, mentally incompetent.

And now?
And now?
Again we may go back in time to when girls
young as fourteen thought about a wire coathanger or drinking
what was it? Was it turpentine?
Or blindfolded being driven to the dark doctor's office
late at night.
And of course being mentally incompetent.
Certainly they should not have a say
in what happens to their life
or any life.

They were married in Reno.
It was a necessary mistake.
Never to be discussed.
Her heart ached and ached, she cried and cried.

AUNT ETHEL AGING

      She shuffles along
Hunched over and shrunken
The walker rattles and squeaks in the once impeccable house
Leaving black marks
Crisscrossing the carpet.

      I don't remember, she mumbles,
I don't remember she mumbles again
Each question about everyday life
Brings the same refrain
I don't remember.

      When we were little, she says
When we were little she muses
And tells a well-remembered childhood story.
The days fade and the old memories
Fill the time.

      We all slept in one room
Three boys on one side of the curtain
Four girls on the other and the baby downstairs
Parents and baby in the tiny living room.

      She gazes off and remembers herself in other times
A farm child helping, too responsible, the oldest of eight
A young bride in love with her alcoholic husband
He was fun, full of pleasure, pain she knew well.
A working woman in the laundry, a childless wife

The days also are filled with childhood
And hour after hour she sits
Old memories, television
Broken by the occasional once-simple task
Now tedious, slow, hard work time-consuming.

Two broken hips and ninety years
Take their toll
And life narrows down
Life narrows down to disappear.

How does it happen she wonders?
And I wonder with her too
Where does the slow creeping come from?
Two aging women separated by 20 years between us.
One sees her future, the other is living it.

Age creeping up on her and on me
Slowly, not always perceptible new wrinkles, new aches
It is there lurking in the night and under the covers
Less energy, an afternoon nap, forgotten words.
Once a luxury now a necessity.

Age a creeping crawling vine,
Caught her by her legs, entangled her arms
Clutches at her waist
And pulls her down toward death
And I follow in her footsteps—

THE DOG ATE MY HOMEWORK

She denied her hair was dyed.

He said he never slept with her.

He said it was not his child.

She claimed to be me.

He said he was 40 and he was 19.

She told me I was wonderful meaning
    she needs a place to stay.

He pretended to like me.

They liked the dinner I served. I didn't.

Playing bridge is learning to lie
    in legitimate helpful ways.

She claimed she had never had a facelift, a buttlift,
    enhanced breasts
    and always was a redhead.

The judge wanted to talk to me about the case,
    but he really wanted
    something else.

                  The Lie

I WALK THE LINE

I walk the line
> The house is dangerous

I walk the line
> One never knows how dangerous

I walk the line
> Sometimes it is almost safe
>
> But never real safe

I walk the line
> I watch carefully
>
> Rigid body; tight lips

I walk the line
> Tension rises
>
> Finally bursts at me
>
> "Where are my scissors?"

I walk the line
> Shrugging my shoulders
>
> "I don't know"
>
> Screaming begins
>
> "Liar liar you always lie"

I walk the line

ALONG THE SILVER ALTAR

Along the silver altar of truth
Wings beat so swiftly they are invisible
Tragedy begins with a radical giver
Your uncle has murdered your father
   and married your mother
You have spent your life writing tragedy for a world
   that does not
      believe in tragedy
Stay calm Stay quiet Fever hasn't learned
   its few bad lines
Called beautiful
Nothing lasts forever
It is all so simple
Is this all there is?
History will end and the sooner the better
Such serious joy
In the desert, on this journey, not once
   not under the stars of promise
God will be crying

To leave the city always takes a quarrel
Raging inside of me
Once a decision was made by beans
2 piles—negative positive
Count the beans—7 negative 3 positive
"Here I will be loved and love"
Puzzled—Is there a price?

I AM WATER FLOWING

I am water flowing down the hill into a lake,
    splashing icy cold and
        deep blue.

I am the sun ever changing moving through
    the sky heating everything
        around me.

I am the wind soft, gently caressing the lovers
    asleep in the hay.

I am the wind blowing through the city
    rattling windows, pushing hard
        against bodies and raising leaves off the ground.

I am the sky blue, blue, blue. Filled with clouds
    snow white or gray
        or black.

I am the earth—

Oh I am the earth deep

The earth all colors—brown to black

yellow to green.

I see. I feel

    Alive—alive

DANCING THROUGH THE TREES

And we play our "understanding game"

nodding our heads—uh-huh—

yes—sure—I see!

As the Indians dance through the trees and no one sees

And the drums beat—and no one hears!

And they chant, and chant

wail and moan—while we play our "understanding game"

We solve the problems that are not the problem
and we chatter chatter—

> Never hearing
>
> Never seeing
>
> Never being
>
> Never moving
>
> —to our own beat—

the heart—our heart—the heart

man's heart—woman's heart

woman's heart—man's heart

BETWEEN

Between clients

On I-80 to anywhere

Beginning drawing

End drawing

In between worlds—

Entering a party

Leaving a party

Sitting alone outside

Walking the hall in school

When I taught Special Ed

Driving to school depressed

Driving home depressed

Moving 60 times

RHYTHMS
"In Harborgate, when I was a kid ..."

Hide the squeaking sickness

The meanness

Drunken violence

Secret sex

Don't be too curious

The pit of my stomach

Unknown loneliness

Manage the fear

Manage the sickness

Manage the hurt

Don't look back

I am delighted for the safety in the beauty
of the sunset that carries me above the street below.
I'm delighted with the low porch
that I secretly climb.

THE POET

when I first met her
I never guessed she was
    a poet
a well respected attorney
    YES

dedicated to self-exploration
living her best life
    YES

one day I heard her read a poem
about her garden
her garden became every garden
    my garden

then I bought her first chapbook
today I opened it again
I stopped and read two poems
    one about her son

one about her as a child
woman wife mother lawyer
    and the girl
running together through
    two pages

listening to her read a poem
    about sand
I smiled, I laughed
my mouth hung open
    endangered sand
    disappearing sand
swallowed up and used to make
    cement

I have her newest book
I read her every day
sometimes the tears slide down
my cheeks in small
rivulets

WORDS AND LANGUAGE
August, 2018

Becoming words I choose

Hearing them, different tones, some with a sneer,

or a laugh, even appreciation

carry more weight, some are discarded

tossed in a pile rotting in the corner

thrown out the window, stomped on, smashed.

Carried to my bosom,

clung to with determination, held tight,

smashed against my ribs,

dripping down my body

Life abandons them, as they cling,

dragged along like a chain.

Walking into the room, a woman,

Looking into eyes, faces wondering,

"What words are those who stare using?"

"Woman" is agreed upon with shrug, a smile

a stare and of course appraisal.

Hard claiming some of the words.
There are words I hold gently
Pull them softly to my heart, hope
sometimes I do actually own them
live them, compassion, gratitude,
kindness, acceptance, not just others, me too.

Beautiful, pushed away hard,
I never hear it.
"Interesting," I accept, worked hard to own.
The meaning is safe. There is a list of
unsafe words, stretching out, stomp on them.

Am I going to reveal this long list?

No, but I will ask if I had lived "beautiful,"
How might I be different?

FLAME

"Well it is and it isn't about two old flames in my life."

The flame blazed
It was an old flame
Soft yellow
Dull orange
Flickering in and out
Now a shining light
Raging, almost escaping
Burning down
Falling away
Blazing again
Red
   Hot
      Dying
Only embers left
Golden against the grate
Shadows creeping
Smoking
   Curling
A brief leap of color
Mellow
  and
      Warm
Cozy
  and
      Bright
It's out.
Blow on it, blow on it
A sigh
re-light
growing bigger
Weak and failing
Scorching hot
   Spreading a steady glow
flame—
old
orange
yellow

flickering
light
raging
burning
fading
blazing
red
hot
dying
embers
golden
shadow
smoking
curling
leaping
mellow
warm
cozy
bright
out
blow
re-light
growing
weak
scorching
spreading
steady
Johnnie
Dean

WORDS
June, 2012

There is something to be acknowledged
Spoken
Filling the room
coloring the air
I breathe.

Not seen, just here.
Even the experience is unseen
known only through my body.

Bodies around me reveal
through waving arms
stamping feet,
smiles, frowns, laughter
moving mouths.

Sounds enter space
Forming shapes, colors,
loud, soft.
If you can hear,
sometimes there is meaning.
If not, well you can make it up.
Your own language.

THE MOUSE AND THE LION
September 4, 2019

The lion roars, prances around announcing his presence
Saying, "I am here."
Big, bold, cannot be missed

Now the mouse hides under his timidity, as he
    scurries around.
Shrinking, hiding, hoping no one sees him

Both hide their murderous rage, pretend anything,
    never acknowledging
The seething rage lying in wait within

Afraid of the revelation, play let's pretend,
    unbecoming they think,
No one wants to see this side

Both with tight teeth choke it back
    as afraid as the mouse and the lion are
of their murderous rage

Both fear more what lurks underneath, pain
    old pain and new barely buried
Protected by layers of murderous rage

And the top layer—the false layer

LOVE
Discovered in an old journal, August 28, 2019

The box is tied tightly closed, waiting for the perfect
Absolute right thing.
The one place, the only place.
Then there is the one perfect right person.

The brain accepts, no rejects
Over and over again and again.
Nothing is just right, perfect.
Deserving enough.

The box sits maybe in the belly,
or close to the heart.
Maybe just out of reach
It grows smaller and smaller
Waiting for the perfect thing
to love
Or the trees, the sun,
an ocean with stars.
walking the earth
looking for the place deserving of love

All beautiful–
Beautiful enough to love?
No one seems to know–
The box darkens

Aren't you supposed to just love
Certain people—family—friends
And then one special person?
A loud roar stops everything.
A roar or a groan coming—
Coming from the direction of the box.

Save it protect it don't let it out.
Nothing is enough
Determined love colors the air,
the sky, everything it touches
Love grows and spreads
Tenderness, light, joy, delight
Everything begins to glow.

THE OLDEST SISTER
August 26, 2012

My mother is gone
The sister above her is gone
Two are left, the oldest and the youngest
Then there is me,
Their oldest niece.

90 years, followed by 82 and then 70.
I watch them both
Curious about my own future.
Their vitality slowly slipping away.
The look of surprise when they move from indoors to out.

I see the puzzled look on their faces,
New stiffness, unexpected pain,
A loss of an old well-established memory
How does it happen they wonder?
And I wonder with them
Where does the slow creeping come?

Three aging women separated by 20 years
One sees her future and the other two are living it.

LOVE STORY

She found a place, frozen grass, icy cold
pulling her blanket tight,
Oh my god! it was cold

Exhausted, sleep found her
the stars dropping low
cold freezing air
startled by unfamiliar warmth
the stars sparkling against a deep dark sky
struggling to free herself from the heavy arm
and yet, not wanting to be free

the warmth of the body cuddled around her
felt too comforting too relaxing
unless she looked at the big hairy hand holding her
felt the bristle of his beard

she fought her fear finally sleep began its slow
creep over her body
the heaviness and the warmth the loud rhythm of his breathing
gratitude brought tears the release
deeply she slept and slept
stars disappearing, sun offering
the day, still cold air
Her bed partner gone searching the landscape

shape appears walking toward her bulky
big husky, wild hair everywhere
too shocked to move she gaped
moving toward her, she saw the man

dark brown eyes peering through all the hair
reaching into a pocket, stale pastry
followed in the other hand holding a paper cup
rich with the smell of coffee eating together
moving toward a river, she followed along
carried her load blanket: plastic bag holds all she owned
where he went she followed
he knew the secrets of the land

the safe camps dangerous one
found the hidden places
for sleep, the daily routines the river
became a bathtub, hidden among reeds
access to backyard gardens
provided vegetables and fruit,
where he asked permission of the watching Gods
picking just what they could use
at the end he bowed hands pressed together
"thank you, thank you" three times

the years passed, patterns developed
that first day continued year after year.
they were watched by the homeless community
were respected by them, loved by them

for the life they had developed of daily routines
mutual regard and the little kindness and the shyness
of their love for each other.
winters were bitter, together under
another tattered blanket replaced each year

by a new tattered blanket
nighttime the same, together.
now, his hairy body silver gray
walking with a heavy limp, slower wanting to just sit
white haired, wrinkled, still following his lead.
The routine was the same, the territory shrunk.

winter came heavy this year together close to the river
they made their bed watching the stars fill the purple blue night sky
sleep crept slowly it was so cold.
finally sleep came after a while again she felt the the bitter cold
she attempted to hang on to some warmth, to sleep

slowly she became aware of the body next to her, no longer warm
her tears came slowly, her breathing filled with gasps
touching, gently smoothing the wild hair,
shivering she sat hands gently moving over him looking at the face
at peace under the heavy beard
finally, she laid curled around him, until she too, was stiff cold

the community found them gently lifted them and carried them close to the fire without speaking washing them with the water warmed on the fire debated about shaving him decided against it combed the hair on his head and his beard laid her next to him, washed her combed her hair, cleaned her fingernails made a circle around them and sang the old fashioned hymns they thought they had forgotten

They were mourned.

I DREAMED I WAS A WILD PONY

I dreamed I was a wild pony
I dreamed I was galloping across a mountain
I dreamed you were on my back
I dreamed I ran and ran carrying you
I dreamed of you again and again
I dreamed you faced me
I dreamed you smiled
I dreamed a tear flooded my eye
I dreamed you touched me gently
I dreamed I sobbed softly
I dreamed the blossom that bloomed
I dreamed the touch I felt on my cheek
I dreamed I was awake
I dreamed I was asleep
I dreamed picture after picture of you
I dreamed you stroked my face
I dreamed I stroked your face and your cheek
I dreamed another land
I dreamed a house
I dreamed the people who lived there
I dreamed you weren't there
I dreamed the dream I did not want
I dreamed I woke up and you were riding a wild pony
    over a hill across the river
I dreamed I watched you become a small fast-moving dot
    on the horizon
I quit riding a wild pony
I quit dreaming
I dreamed my heart was beating full of feeling.

MISSING AND FORGETTING
May 1, 2018

I will miss the sunlight through the trees.
>> the brilliance of fall, rust, red, orange and gold
> the bare branches against the sky.

I will remember the wonder of watching one lone leaf fall.

I will miss the sound of the wind blowing around the house.
>> the crashing of waves against the rocks
> the sun setting, reflecting on the water.

I will remember the awe of seeing the ocean for the first time.

I will miss the lush hills of spring.
>> the summer-parched hills
> the first snowfall.

I will remember the serenity and quiet as the snow piled higher and higher.

I will miss the sunrise when I wake in the morning.
>> the sunset over the trees
> the blue of the sky and the clouds.

I will remember driving watching the sun set on one side, the moon rise on the other.

I will miss the full moon in the fall.
>> the new moon in a winter sky
> the changing moon from no moon to full moon.

I will remember a cat my family named Moonie, because the moon followed us home.

I will miss the solstice, both summer and winter.
> miss the longest day now getting shorter.
> miss the shortest day now getting longer.

I will remember the seasons of life.

I will miss beautiful music.
> soaring voices and violins playing
> the soprano at operas.

I will remember the tears of hearing a beautiful song played or sung.

I will miss having coffee and the paintings on the wall.
> the vibrant colors of the paint
> the feel of a brush gliding over paper.

I will remember the thrill of color and brush.

I will miss the moment of finishing a wonderful book.
> the emotional impact of a book on my soul
> the visions created while reading.

I will remember the longing in my heart to create something, anything.

I will miss this earth and the smell of it.
> the feel and the look of this earth
> the beauty of this planet.

I hope I remember somewhere and sometime what it meant to be here.

THE BLACK FEDORA AND OTHER THINGS

Red, yellow, orange tulips dance and bob.

Blend into a wash of color only to be lost from vision.

Pain emerges old, rancid, sour.

The taste lies in my mouth and I spit into my cheeks, suck on my teeth to rid myself of it.

I'm anxious and the color leaves—too much chaos, too much confusion turns gray and I want color, solid color, bright to give my inside feeling of warmth of life.

And the birds dance their dance, long-legged knobby knees, too thin for their puffed up body.

I sit with the old sour rancid taste of pain.

The memories are gone; there's just the taste.

The birds move in dances slow, fast, graceful, and clumsy. I know the movement.

Old feelings live in different places.

Gone are the dark corners, the red-hot burn now it's just a taste in my mouth.

The puffin saunters by.

Smug puffed up unconcerned about feelings;
fears, darkness, old jealousies and I sit in them,
open to them, tasting them, not rejecting them.
The night is cold and the horse neighs in her field
filled with sad and lonely.

Now it leaves my chest sad and lonely and reminds me of the new place the old feelings.

Swans and geese pass me by swimming and honking crying their cry, deep and strong.

I gaze at them and feel it slip into my belly deep and strong from the swans and from the geese.

I notice the man.
I notice the cocky hat.
I notice the black fedora.
I sit and stare.

He dances by doing a jig or some jazz or maybe a little swing.

Everywhere are dancers.

The old rancid taste fades.

Shy lonely fades deep and strong fades and
the old horse is quiet in the field.

Gratitude arrives on the wings of birds.

Gratitude arrives in an old horse and song.

Gratitude arrives in a black fedora.

Acknowledgments

The following is a list of all those who got this book ready for publishing and those who supported me and helped me so it was not totally impossible at age 93.

Jan Tannarome, who kept me in line, improving my mind with her listening and editing of the book. My gratitude to you.

Kit Bailey, who was proofreader, editor, and great support. He did an excellent job, and was kind and thoughtful throughout the entire endeavor. I cannot sing his praises enough, or express my gratitude enough!

Julie Valin, who has helped with the publishing process. She has been generous with her skills and our working together has been a delight.

Anne Adden is the most recent member of the group. Anne's design skills, talents and creativity enhanced all the activities involved in getting the book published.

All of these people enriched my life, improved my writing and brought joy to the process.

In addition, I would like to add my children: Char Ghio, Beth Thompson, and Tony Ghio; my grandchildren Nicole and Taylor Thompson, and my great-grandchildren, Ava, Cairo and Judah Ubaka. To all of you, be loved and blessed, and have many moments of happiness.

Thanks to the Unitarian Universalist Community of the Mountains and my many friends there. All of you hold a place in my heart. May you be blessed with love and wisdom.

May Susan Suntree be blessed. She reminded me every day to write the first book and now here she is, still in my life, encouraging me, keeping me on track and inspiring me by her dedication to her own work.

www.ingramcontent.com/pod-product-compliance
Lightning Source LLC
Chambersburg PA
CBHW031322160426
43196CB00007B/628